# DOODLE
# SKETCHBOOK

## ART JOURNALING
## FOR BOYS

D1016205

DAWN DeV...

**GIBBS SMITH**
TO ENRICH AND INSPIRE HUMANKIND

FOR MY ENTIRE FAMILY,
ESPECIALLY MY MOTHER,
EVELYN, AND MY BROTHER,
RON, WHO ALWAYS BELIEVE
IN AND SUPPORT ME.

Manufactured in Shenzhen, China in September 2011 by Toppan Printing Company

First Edition
15 14 13 12 11     5 4 3 2 1

Text and Illustrations © 2011 Dawn DeVries Sokol

Published by
Gibbs Smith
P.O. Box 667
Layton, Utah 84041

1.800.835.4993 orders
www.gibbs-smith.com
www.dblogala.com

Designed by Dawn DeVries Sokol
Printed and bound in China
Gibbs Smith books are printed on either recycled, 100% post-consumer waste, FSC-certified papers or on paper produced from a 100% certified sustainable forest/controlled wood source.

ISBN 13: 978-1-4236-2046-4

# PLEASE RETURN TO:

**NAME:**

**ADDRESS:**

**PHONE:**

**E-MAIL:**

# ART JO

You might see their sid...

## HERE'S WHAT YOU NEED TO GET STARTED IN DOODLE SKETCHBOOK:

- **pens**
  Use all kinds of pens. Find ones that work for YOU.

- **COLLAGE**
  Cut up some of the backgrounds, words, and doodles at the back of this sketchbook and use them for collage or paste them around the sides of the pages as borders then add on to them!

- **PHOTOS AND XEROX**
  Cut out and paste in copies of photos of family and friends. Used magazines also work great for images of people and

objects. Turn the magazine upside down
while flipping through to see patterns
and shapes you might not see otherwise.

## • CuT aNd PasTe
Try different ways of pasting and
attaching items to pages, such as
different tapes, staples, brads, stickers,
labels, photo corners...

## • HANDWRITING
Mixing words with visuals is fun!
Write down words and stories in your
sketchbook, too.

# FOUND ART

If you don't like your own hand-writing, there are some ready-doodled words at the back of the sketchbook. You can also cut out words and letters from used magazines and junk mail, or print out words from your computer on different papers.

# RUBBER STAMPS

Alphabet rubber stamps are a great way to "write" in your sketchbook, too! Ink pads come in all different colors.

# OUTLINING

Try outlining images you paste down. If you're working on a colored page, use a pen, marker, or crayon that will match that color. This blends the image into the page.

# TIPS:

- If you make a mistake, just doodle or collage over it. Mistakes usually lead to better art.

- Tool Tips are included throughout as suggestions. Follow or ignore them—it's up to you!

- Let your mind wander as you doodle. You never know what great ideas will pop up.

# HAVE FUN!

# tools

## TO USE

### COLORED PENCILS
of any kind should work.

### WATERCOLOR PENCILS
These look like colored pencils
except they can turn into watercolor
on the page. Simply color on the
page then use a wet
paintbrush or wet
your fingertip and
smudge in. You can
also dip the pencil
tip in water and
color that way.

### NUMBER 2 PENCILS
are great, too!

## BLACK PENS

There are all kinds: Micron, Prismacolor, and Pitt Pens. Play with different kinds.

## GEL PENS

Available in craft, art, and office supply stores, these pens leave great color on your pages. Use them to fill in doodles.

Gel pens are sold in a wide variety, such as Soufflé pens that are pastel colored and puff up a little on the page when dry. The Soufflé pen is a great opaque gel pen and shows up well on dark papers. Other gel pens include Moonlights (which are neon colored and more opaque), Glaze, Gelly Roll Metallic, Gelly Roll Stardust, and more.

## BIC OR SHARPIE PENS

These pens are good and come in a wide variety of colors, although they CAN bleed through to the other side of the paper.

## CRAYOLA PIP SQUEAKS

The Pip Squeaks work well—colors are more like watercolor, not as bright as other pens, and shouldn't bleed through paper. They're widely available and CHEAP!

## CRAYONS

I like crayons, too, as a last touch—for drawing borders around images and adding color.

## PORTFOLIO OIL PASTELS BY CRAYOLA

These work like watercolor pencils. Use them as a last touch—trying to draw over these with any pen will only stop up the pen. You can smear portfolio oil pastels into the paper using your fingertip. Or use a bit of water.

# WAYS TO ATTACH iTeMS

GLUE STiCK

Less messy than regular glue

Paper Clips

tape

Scotch or masking tape:
Use on corners of items
or all around edges

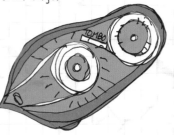

Any dry roller
tape glue also works

## YOU ALSO NEED:

* A pair of small
scissors to make
cutting out tiny
items easy

* 1 or 2 cheap
paintbrushes

DOODLING WITH **ink SPLOTCHES**

Ink splatters make a great starting point for doodles. Doodle around the splotches with pens or make your own ink splotches. Go for it—fill the page!

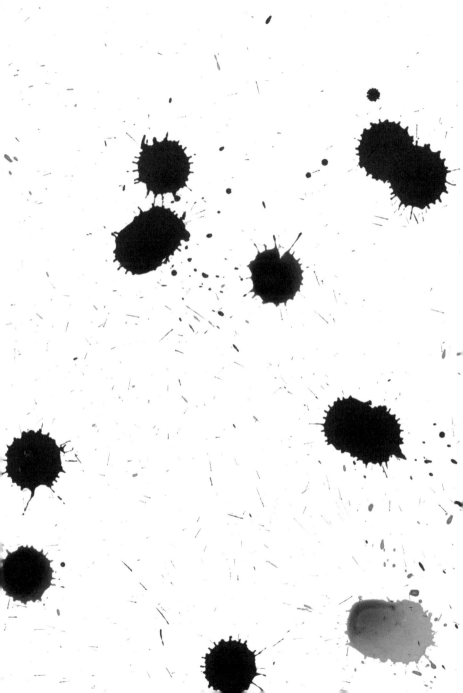

Treat these pages as a blank wall.
Place different papers and scraps down
on the pages and then doodle over them
in graffiti style!

GO GRA

# URBAN
## ALPHABET

Doodle an alphabet that looks graffiti or urban style to you. This is yours to use from now on!

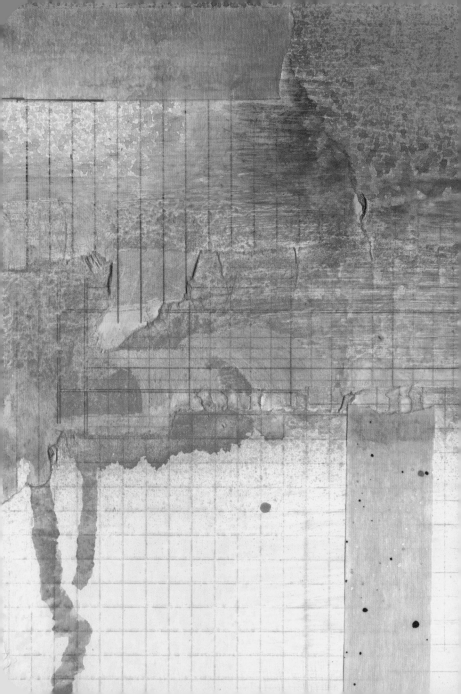

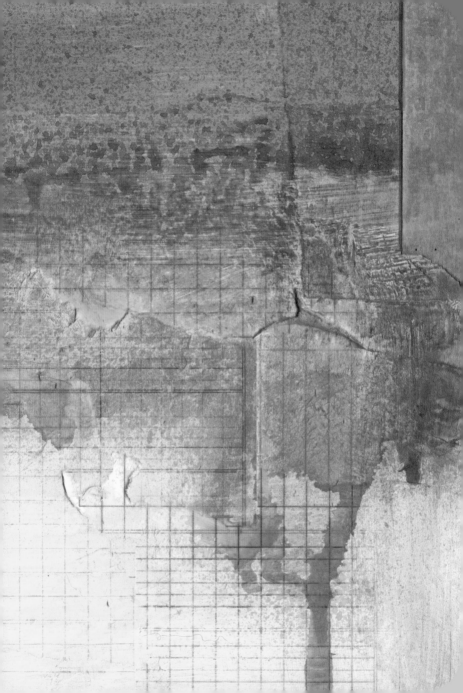

# ROCKiN' the IPOD

Even if you don't have an MP3 player
or an iPod, you can still deck it out!

## TiP

ONE WAY IS TO TAPE IT
OVER WITH DUCT TAPE IN
VARIOUS COLORS, THEN
DOODLE OVER THAT.

You've found an important piece of evidence.

Make sure to note and DOODLE everything!

DATE:

TIME:

LOCATION:

NOTES:

- - - - - - - - - - - - - - - - - - - - - - - - - - - -

OFFICIAL USE ONLY:

THIS CAN BE ANYTHING—MAYBE
A RECEIPT FROM LUNCH, A CANDY
WRAPPER, OR A MOVIE OR CONCERT
TICKET STUB. ATTACH IT WITH A
PAPER CLIP OR STAPLE TO ADD
DIMENSION.

# TUNE-AGE

Write down some of the words from your favorite song, doodle around them, then add the colors it brings to mind. What does this song make you think of?

Find a photo and paste
it down. Doodle.

SINGER/GROUP:

# BUGGIN'

Like bugs and insects? Doodle them! You
could even create some imaginary bugs...

GLUE STICK

TiP:
CUT OUT A PHOTO OF
AN INSECT FROM A
MAGAZINE, PASTE IT
DOWN, AND DRAW MORE
INSECTS FROM THAT.

# SURF'S UP

And so is the snow and the cement!

Time to doodle YOUR designs on a surfboard, skateboard, and snowboard.

Two templates are included for each board, one for the front, and one for the back.

 TRY TO MAKE EACH DESIGN DIFFERENT.
ONE WAY IS TO MAKE YOUR DOODLES
ABOUT SURFING, SNOWBOARDING, OR
SKATEBOARDING, SUCH AS DOODLES
ABOUT THE OCEAN FOR SURFING, ETC.

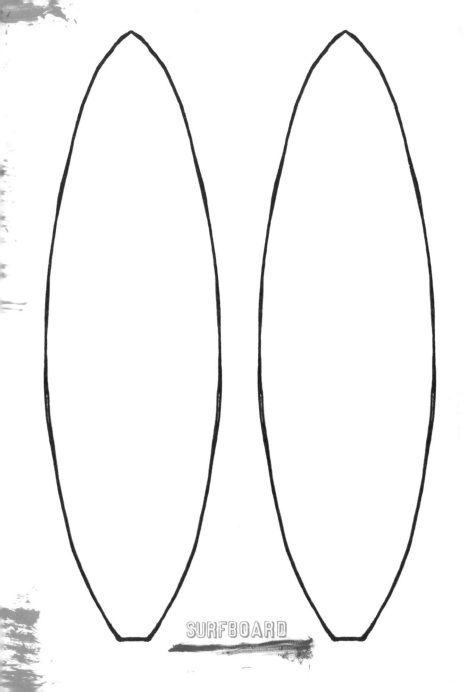

SURFBOARD

SKATEBOARD

SNOWBOARD

# THUMBIN' IT

Either press your thumbs onto an ink pad or color them with a marker and then press them down on the page to create thumbprints. Doodle over them and around them to create all kinds of things!

**TiP:**

IF YOU'RE COLORING YOUR THUMBS
WITH MARKERS TO MAKE THE PRINTS,
TRY USING MORE THAN ONE COLOR
ON EACH THUMB. MAKE STRIPES OF
COLORS OR DOTS OF COLORS.

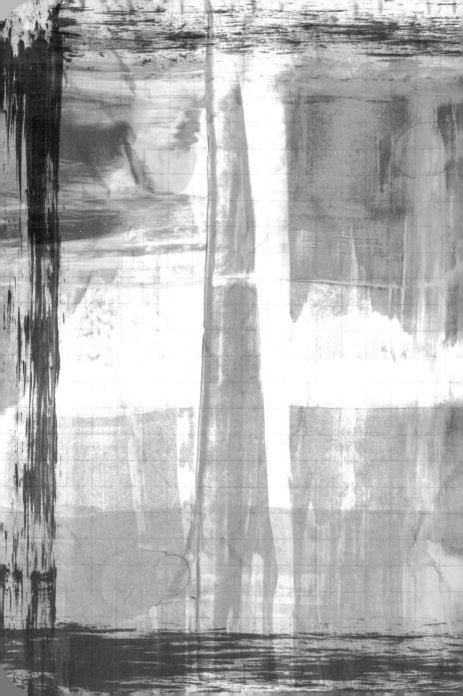

# DOODLED DROIDS

R2-D2, C-3PO, Optimus Prime, Megatron, Wall-E ... which robot is YOUR favorite? If a robot doesn't come to mind, create one of your own.

# MANGA▰

Doodle your typical day as a comic strip.

# MANIA

If you could doodle
anything on your bedroom
wall, what would it be?

WALL
DOODLE

LEFTY-

# RIGHTY

If you are right-handed, doodle on
these pages using only your left hand.
If you are left-handed, doodle on these
pages using only your right hand.

Paste photos here or list their
names and doodle around them.

# TODAY I AM:

Find a recent picture of you and photocopy it. Now paste the photocopy down on this page. How are you feeling today? What do you need to do today? Write it and doodle it all over this page.

**TOOL TiP:**

TO CUT OUT PEOPLE FROM PHOTOS, USE SMALL SCISSORS TO GET IN TINY CREVICES. THE SMALLER POINT HELPS TO CUT IN NARROW AREAS.

# MY COLORS

What's your color palette? Scribble those colors here.

You might see their side

You might see their side

# WHAT
# A SCENE

Mix photos and collage with doodles to make your own "scene", whether it be real or something imagined.

# ODE TO HIGH TOPS

Doodle a design
on a pair of sneakers,
using the outlines here.

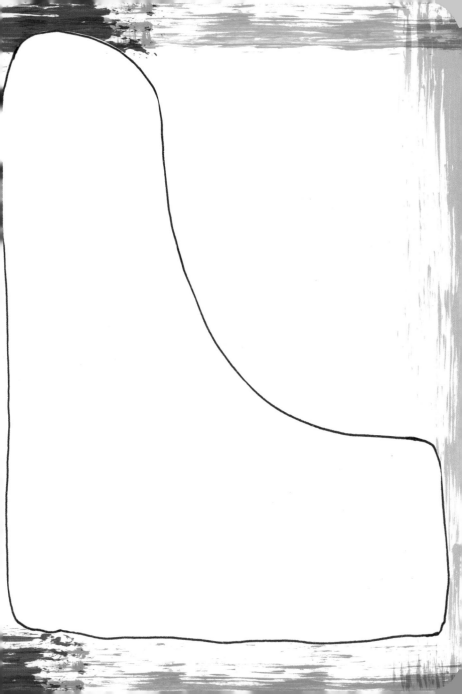

# I LIKE TO EAT...

Doodle, collage, and list your fave foods.

# ALL ARO

Look around you right now. What do you see? List it out then doodle it!

# UND ME

TOOL TiP:

USE A LABEL MAKER HERE TO "LABEL" WHAT YOU SEE, LIKE EVIDENCE.

# THINGS I SAID TODAY:

1)

2:

3

1→

2>

3]

THINGS I WISH I HAD SAID INSTEAD:

→ whAT i

LEARNED TODAY

# MAP IT OUT

[Where did you go today? Draw it as a map on these pages.]

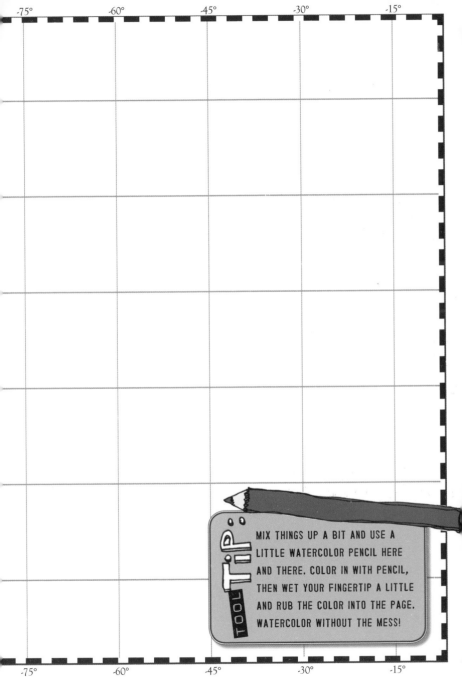

TOOL TiP

MIX THINGS UP A BIT AND USE A
LITTLE WATERCOLOR PENCIL HERE
AND THERE. COLOR IN WITH PENCIL,
THEN WET YOUR FINGERTIP A LITTLE
AND RUB THE COLOR INTO THE PAGE.
WATERCOLOR WITHOUT THE MESS!

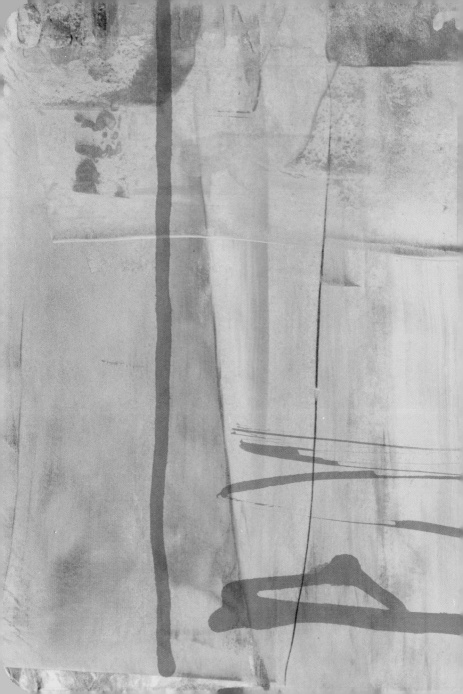

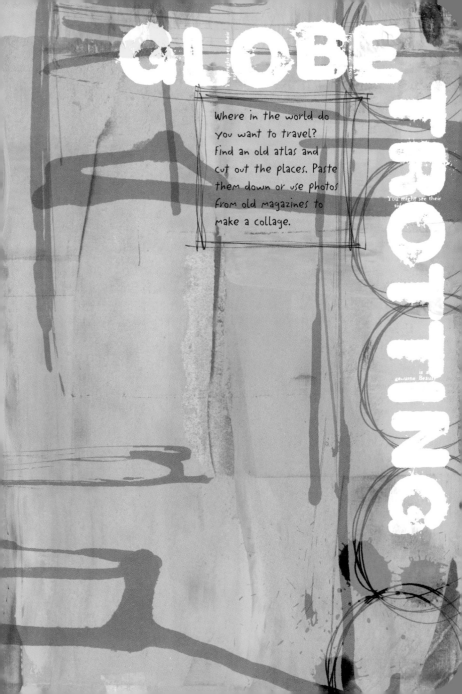

# GLOBE TROTTING

Where in the world do
you want to travel?
Find an old atlas and
cut out the places. Paste
them down or use photos
from old magazines to
make a collage.

Doodle on these pages using just a regular No. 2 pencil
but DON'T erase any of it.

# PHOTO FINISH

Find some photos of you
and your friends or you and
your family. Paste one down
and try to doodle out the
scene from the photo to fill
the rest of the page.

**TiP:** IF YOU WANT TO USE YOUR
FAVORITE PHOTOS OVER AGAIN,
MAKE PHOTOCOPIES TO USE IN
THIS SKETCHBOOK.

Cut out your favorite monsters, aliens, or creatures from magazines, posters, or old comic books. Tape them down with masking tape or duct tape to make a collage.

# >ZOMBIE

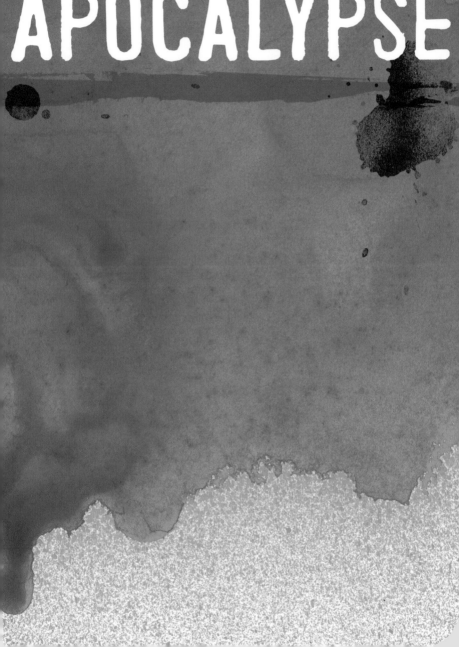

If you could be someone famous, who would you be and why? A rock star, super hero, reality star, sports star? Find a photo of them. Doodle and write about it.

# ALMOST FAMOUS

# FLICK
# PICKS

Comment on movies you see. Add ticket stubs, photos from ads, etc.

LIKE

is a

Maxime Beauty

ing water, fruit

good);

WHAT DO YOU SEE IN THIS BACKGROUND? DOODLE FROM IT!

Use masking tape and/or duct tape to paste down some found objects. Fill in the space on the pages with tape and then doodle over and around all of it!

# GOT GAME?

football, basketball, soccer?
What's YOUR sport? Use these
pages to collage it, doodle it,
and write about it.

Use junk mail, a ticket stub, a wrapper, a paper cup—anything! Don't throw it away. Instead, art it up! Doodle around it. Fill the whole page with recycled items. Maybe it's just a big collage of stuff.

# HANDS UP!

Place your nondrawing hand on the page and trace around it. Now fill it with doodles and color it in.

# MAKING

What's going on in the world around you? Cut out headlines from newspapers, magazines, or printouts of online news and paste them here.

# HEADLINES

# MY PEEPS

Paste down photos of your friends, then doodle and write why they are important to you. Use the frames or collage them ALL over the page.

TOOL TiP:

CRAYON

USE A PORTFOLIO CRAYON TO LIGHTLY
OUTLINE THE PHOTOS AND PIECES
YOU PASTE DOWN. SMEAR IT INTO THE
PAPER WITH YOUR FINGERTIP.

# Doodles of My

What happened today? Doodle and write about it!
Make sure to write the date somewhere, too.

Day

# STUFF I LIKE

PASTE down all kinds of images from magazines, labels, etc. and then DOODLE all over them.

# FAVE CLASS SUBJECT

LEAST FAVE CLASS SUBJECT

5 COOL

THINGS

COLLAGED

You might see their

♥ALPHABET-

Find different letters from old magazines to form an ALPHABET.

DOODLE over them to make the letters your own.

Doodle using only markers
on these pages.

make my
MARK:

.

WHAT I FOUND

THIS WEEK

Create a board game
or write an idea
for a video game on
these pages.

GAME ON

Doodle, write, or add paper or flat items from each day.
Make sure to include the date and what you did that day.

# A WEEK
# IN MY LIFE

**SUNDAY**

**MONDAY**

**TUESDAY**

WEDNESDAY

THURSDAY

FRIDAY

SATURDAY

# On My Music Player

(Draw your music player—MP3, iPod, etc. List, doodle, or collage some of your favorite songs that are on it.)

SPILL

Using a black Sharpie, let loose on these pages and write something you did or something you like or want.

scr

TiP FIND PORTIONS OF PHOTOS OF BUILDINGS, PATTERNS, OR GRAPH PAPER AND USE THEM AS A HAPHAZARD COLLAGE BASE, THEN SCRIBBLE YOUR CITYSCAPE OVER IT.

BBLE A CITYSCAPE

# DOODLE AND COLLAGE A SCI-FI WORLD

# MY FUTURE SELF

What do you want to be in life?
List careers you want to explore.

CREATURE

Either paste down  photos of your pet or doodle your pet on these two pages. If you don't have a pet, draw your dream pet. Add its name, food bowl, collar, favorite sleeping spot, or other details.

FEATURE

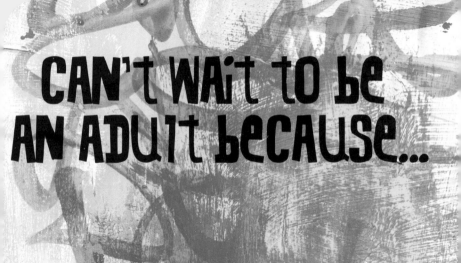

# CAN'T WAIT TO BE AN ADULT BECAUSE...

MY FAVORITE
PLACE TO BE...

Cover this page with stickers. Doodle around or over them.

# STICK IT!

# Doodle on a Chalkboard

TOOL **TiP:**

USE A WITE-OUT PEN, A WHITE
SOUFFLÉ PEN, OR A WHITE SHARPIE
PAINT PEN ON THESE PAGES.

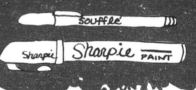

# buiLdiNG
## CHARACTER

You're in charge of developing a new cartoon for TV. You need to create the main character. Draw your character in all different poses with all kinds of expressions.

**TiP:**

THINK WILD! MAYBE IT'S
SHAPED DIFFERENTLY THAN
REGULAR BILLS AND COINS AND
CONTAINS WILD COLORS.

# CHA-CHING!

Doodle and create
your own money!

"CARVE" DOODLES IC

USE A BUTTER KNIFE TO PRESS
IN YOUR DOODLE PATTERNS
WITHOUT CUTTING THROUGH
THE PAPER. COLOR OVER THESE
MARKS WITH A PEN OR PENCIL.

TO YOUR DESKTOP

## TOP SECRET/CONFIDENTIAL:

Create a pocket on the page and doodle and write something you don't want anyone to know about yourself. Tuck into the pocket.

**TiP:**
GLUE DOWN THREE SIDES OF
A PIECE OF PAPER, SO IT
FORMS THE POCKET.

# Pencil Me In

Use only colored pencils to doodle on these pages.

# [ TO A "T" ]

Design your own T-shirt.

FRONT

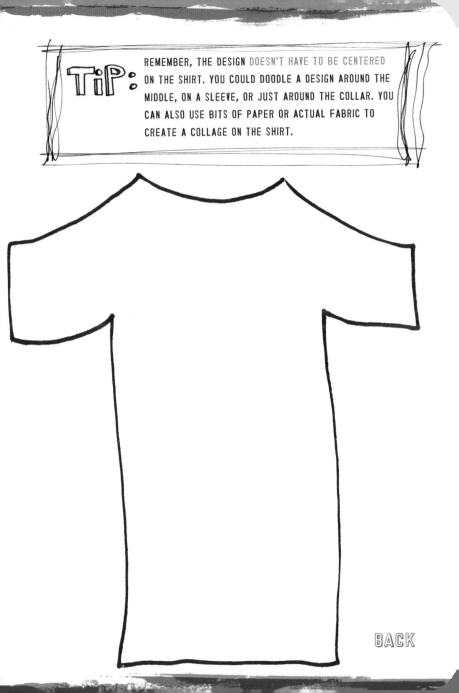

**TiP:** REMEMBER, THE DESIGN DOESN'T HAVE TO BE CENTERED ON THE SHIRT. YOU COULD DOODLE A DESIGN AROUND THE MIDDLE, ON A SLEEVE, OR JUST AROUND THE COLLAR. YOU CAN ALSO USE BITS OF PAPER OR ACTUAL FABRIC TO CREATE A COLLAGE ON THE SHIRT.

BACK

D E F G H I J K L M

Q R S T U V W X Y Z

e f g h i j k l m n o p q r s t

1 2 3 4 5 6 7 8 9 0

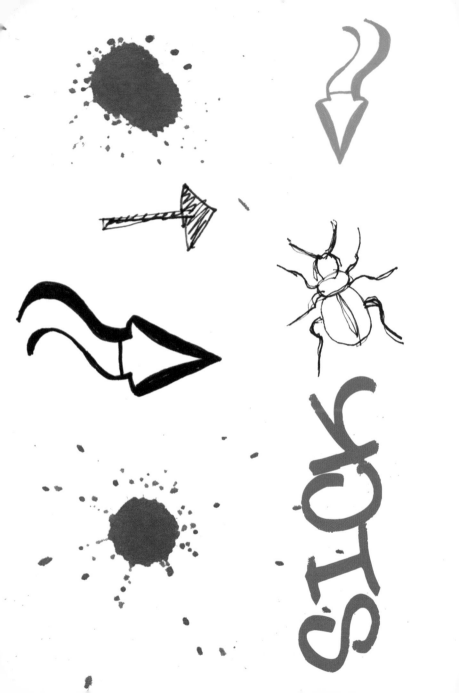

DOOM

HIP

BUGGIN'

SCORE

HOP

ROCK ON

# ZOMBIE

## HELLO
### my name is